TÜRKIYE

Written by Doug Barone

COUNTRIES of the WORLD

PowerKiDS press

Published in 2025
by The Rosen Publishing Group, Inc.
2544 Clinton Street, Buffalo, NY 14224

Written by: Doug Barone
Edited by: Elise Carraway
Designed by: Miranda Tremere

Cataloging-in-Publication Data

Names: Barone, Doug.
Title: Türkiye / Doug Barone.
Description: Buffalo, NY : PowerKids Press, 2025. | Series: Countries of the world | Includes glossary and index.
Identifiers: ISBN 9781499449310 (pbk.) | ISBN 9781499449327 (library bound) | ISBN 9781499449334 (ebook)
Subjects: LCSH: Turkey--Juvenile literature.
Classification: LCC DR417.4 B376 2025 | DDC 956.1--dc23

Manufactured in the United States of America

CPSIA Compliance Information: Batch #CW25PK. For further information contact Rosen Publishing at 1-800-237-9932.

Find us on

Image Credits

All images are courtesy of Shutterstock.com, unless otherwise specified. With thanks to Getty Images, Thinkstock Photo and iStockphoto. Cover – sadullahkisi, mama_mia, Ella_Ca, Anna Kosheleva, GoodStudio. 2 – Nejdet Duzen. 4–5 – Andrew Minsk, Wangkun Jia. 6–7 – Volha Vasilevich, Selcuk Oner. 8–9 – muratart, Gatot Adri. 10–11 – Drazen Zigic, Pixel-Shot. 12–13 – memedozaslanphotography, noowans. 14–15 – Stoktur, nurdem atay. 16–17 – Nadezhda Bolotina, Zurijeta. 18–19 – photoyh, thomas koch. 20–21 – Feel good studio, YusufAslan. 22–23 – muratart, Drazen Zigic.

CONTENTS

Words that look like <u>this</u> can be found in the glossary on page 24.

WHERE IS TÜRKIYE?

Türkiye is a country that sits on two continents called Asia and Europe. It is surrounded by both land and sea.

Türkiye's official language is Turkish. Many people live in large cities, such as Istanbul and Ankara.

The capital city of Türkiye is Ankara.

LANDSCAPE AND WEATHER

The climate changes across the country, but it is usually cooler near the coast. Many tourists visit Türkiye in the summer to enjoy the hot weather.

Türkiye has many different landscapes. It has very long coastlines, large lakes, high mountain peaks, and grassy fields.

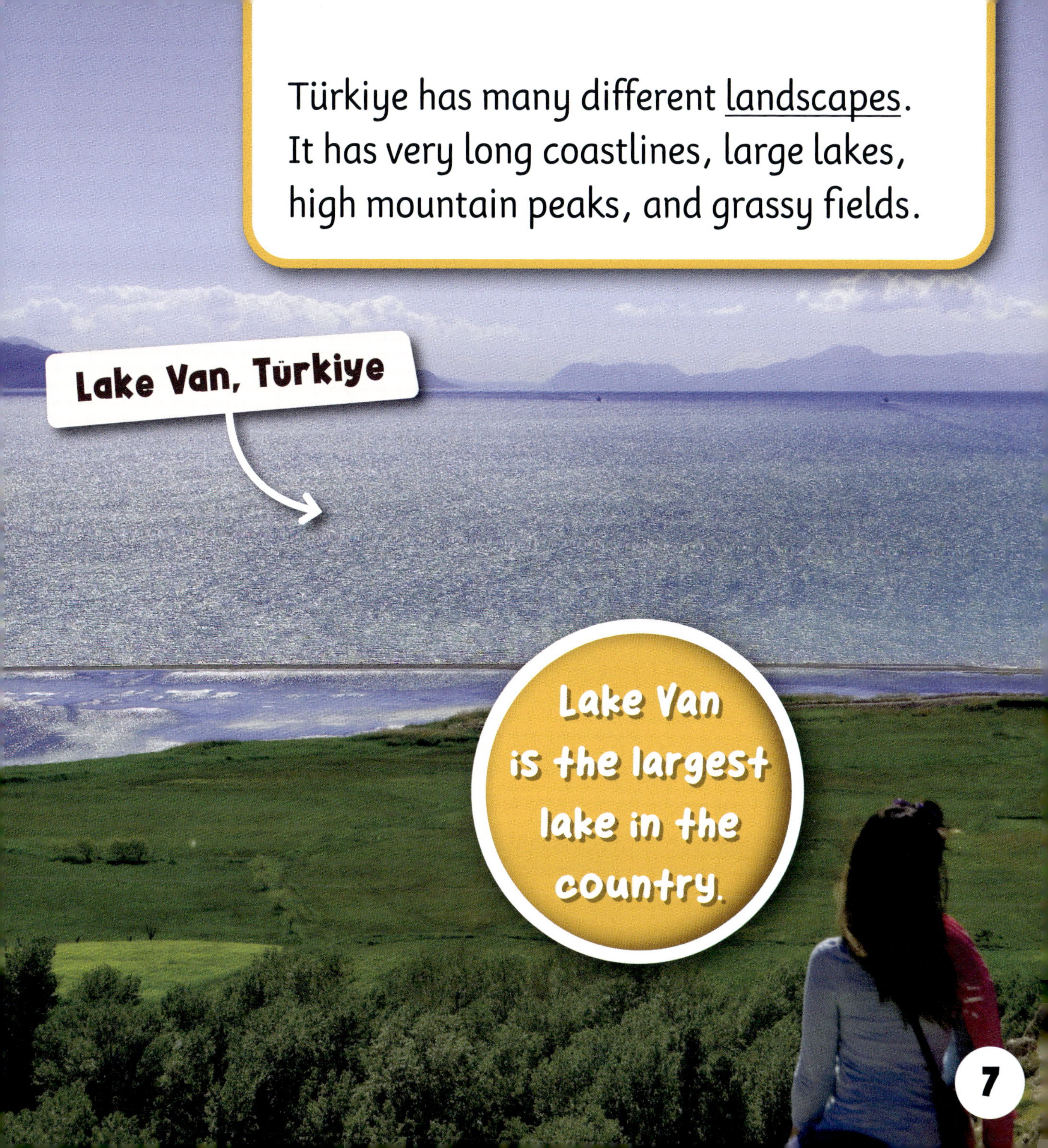

Lake Van is the largest lake in the country.

RELIGION

The religion with the most followers in Türkiye is Islam. People who follow Islam are called Muslims. Their place of worship is called a mosque.

The Sultan Ahmed Mosque, Istanbul

Shoes must be taken off when entering a mosque.

Muslims must wash their hands and feet before entering a mosque to pray. This is a sign of respect to Allah.

FAMILIES

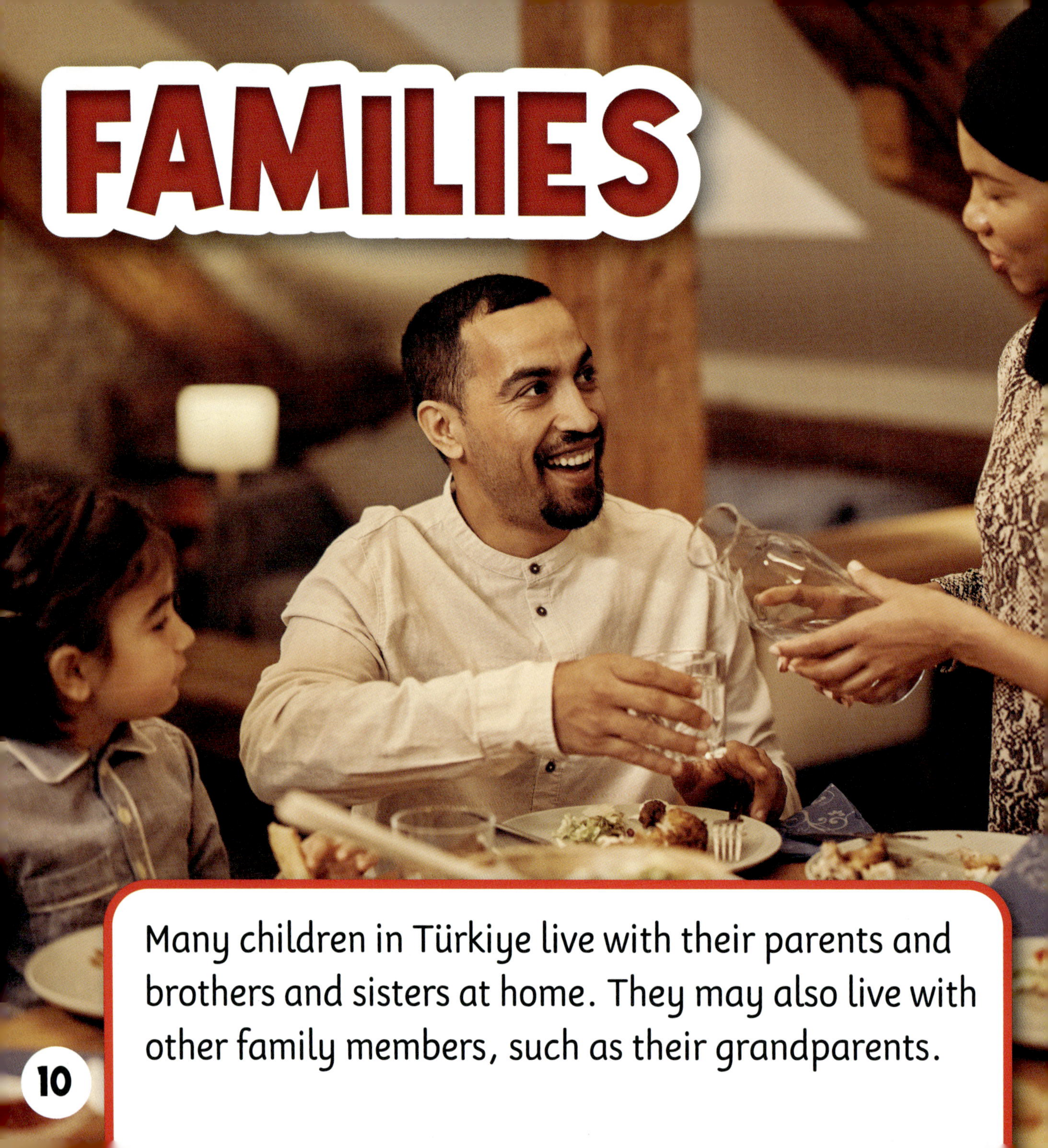

Many children in Türkiye live with their parents and brothers and sisters at home. They may also live with other family members, such as their grandparents.

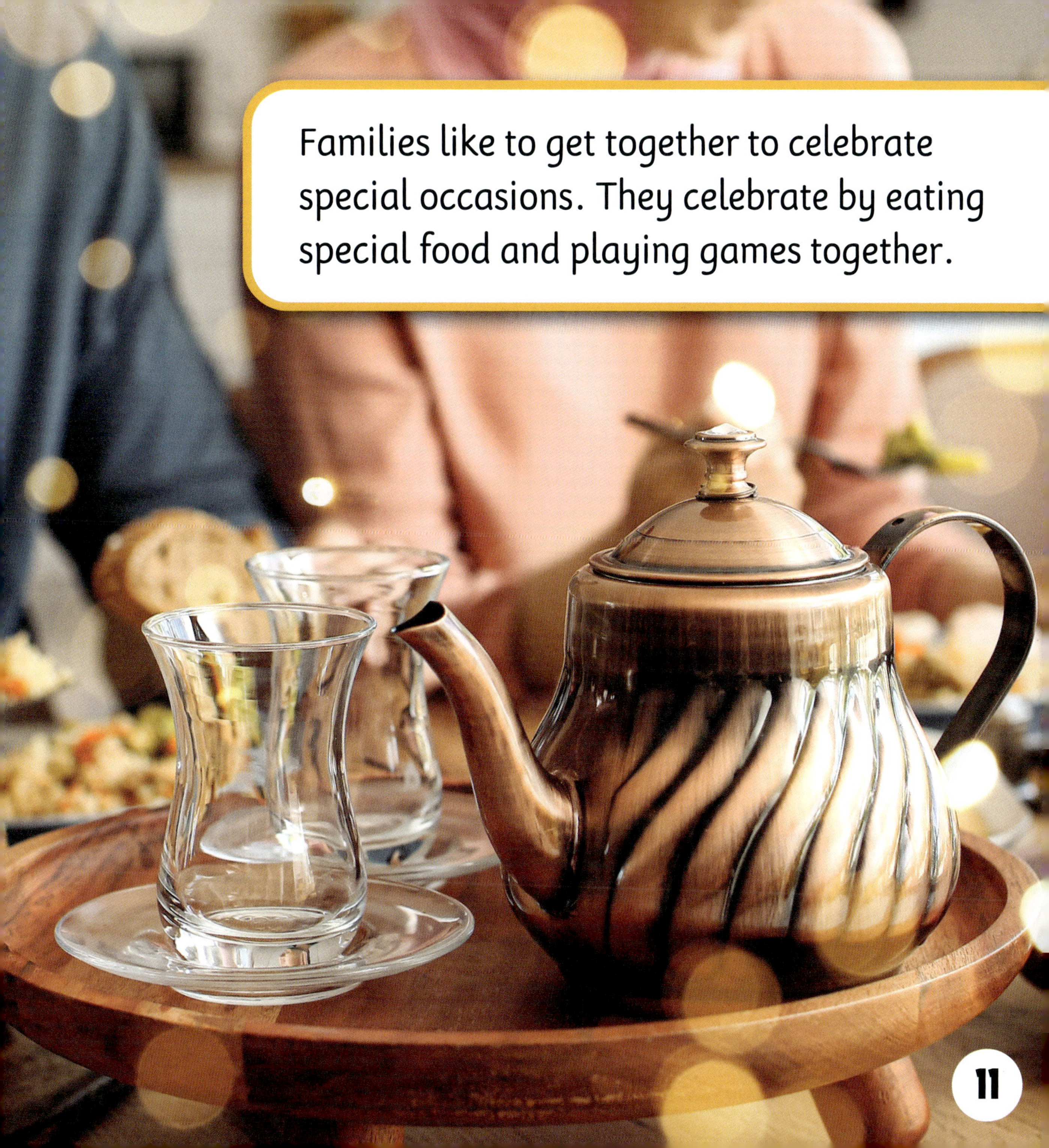

Families like to get together to celebrate special occasions. They celebrate by eating special food and playing games together.

SCHOOL

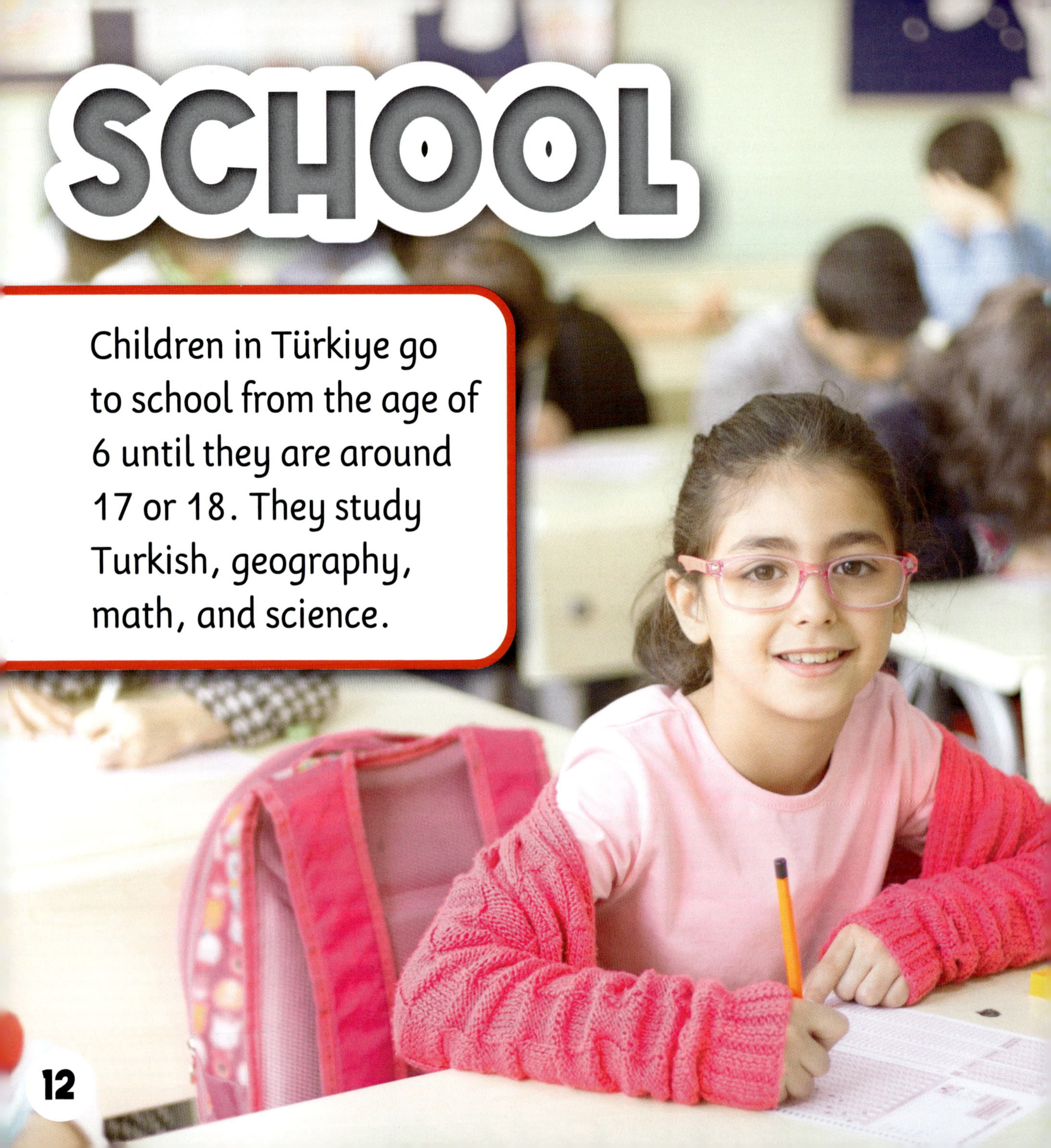

Children in Türkiye go to school from the age of 6 until they are around 17 or 18. They study Turkish, geography, math, and science.

Children also have to study another language. The most common language to study is English. They can also study German, French, or another language.

HOME

In Türkiye's large cities, such as Istanbul and Ankara, many families live together in big buildings called apartments.

There are also lots of people who live in small villages and towns, where there are many fields to farm.

CLOTHING

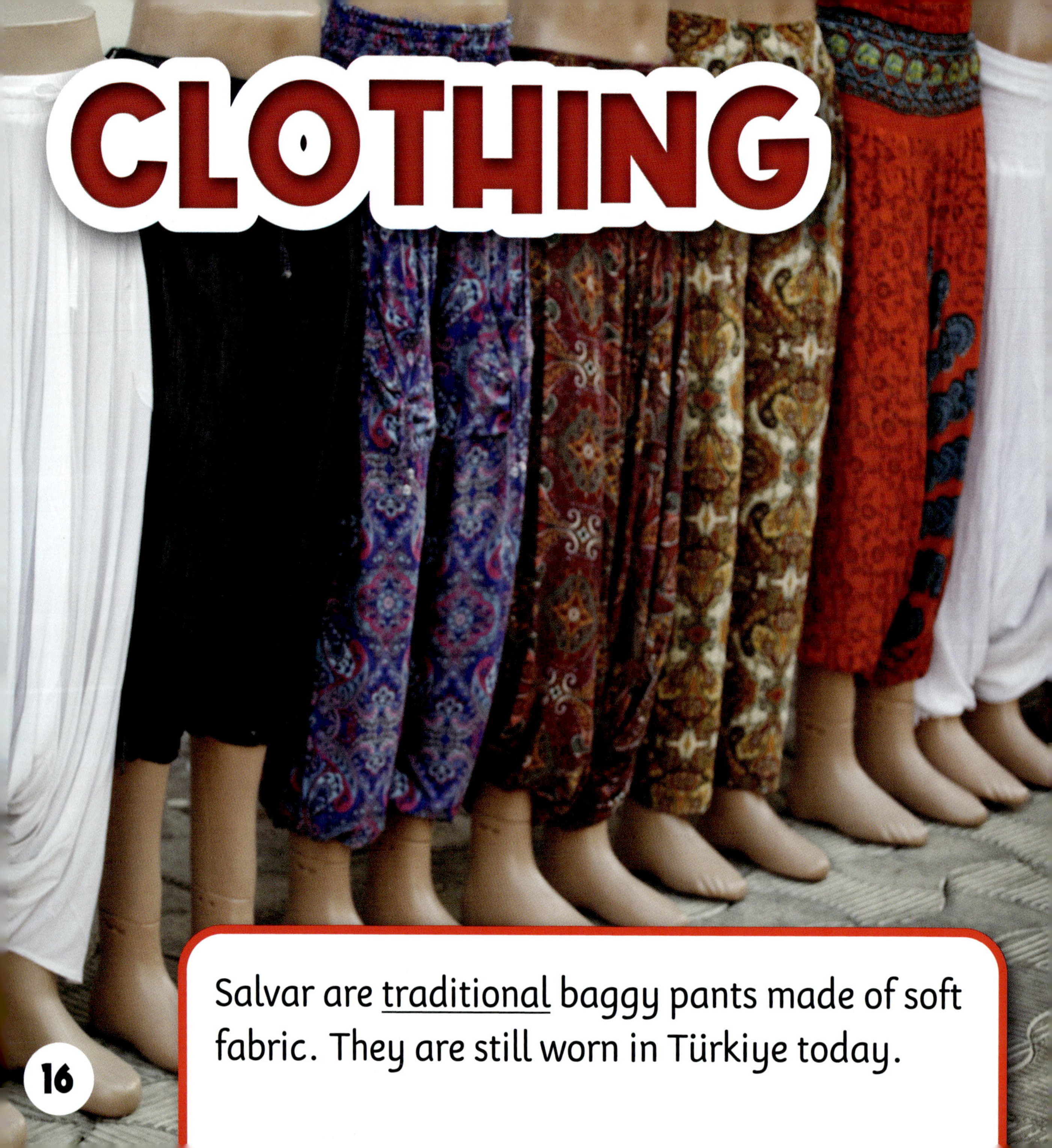

Salvar are traditional baggy pants made of soft fabric. They are still worn in Türkiye today.

People in Türkiye also wear modern clothing. They may wear loose, comfortable dresses or shorts in summer to keep cool.

SPORTS

Soccer is the most popular sport in Türkiye. Many fans go to watch soccer to support their favorite team.

Other popular sports in Türkiye include volleyball and basketball. Many children learn how to play some of these sports at school.

FOOD

The kebab is one of Türkiye's most popular dishes. Meat is placed onto a skewer and is grilled over a hot charcoal fire. Traditionally, the meat is lamb, but other kinds of meat can be used.

Baklava is a famous Turkish dessert. It is made from layers of pastry with chopped nuts and held together with syrup or honey.

FUN FACTS

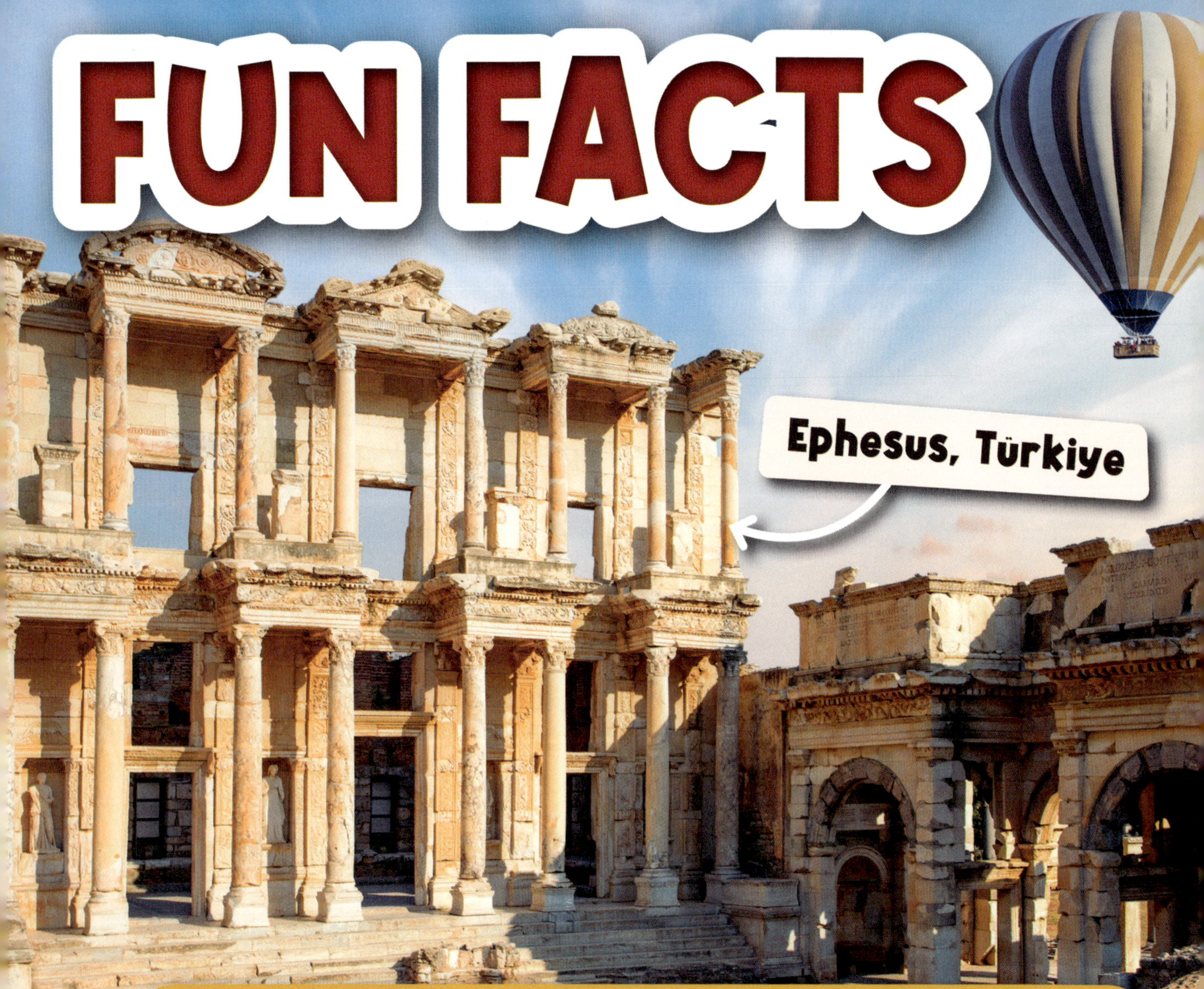

Millions of tourists visit Türkiye every year. They go to see the amazing landscapes and historic sites, such as the ancient Greek city of Ephesus.

Traditional Turkish stories are full of magical creatures, such as dragons and genies. There are hundreds of fairy tales that are still told to children today.

GLOSSARY

climate the weather in a large area

coast where the land meets the sea

continents large areas of land that are usually made up of many countries

landscapes the physical features of different areas of land

modern to do with recent or present times

official to do with something that is recognized as having power or being important

religion a system of faith and worship, especially to do with a god or gods

tourists people who visit another place for pleasure

traditional to do with beliefs, customs, or ways of behaving that have been around for a long time

worship religious acts of praise, such as prayer

INDEX